What Is Germ Theory?

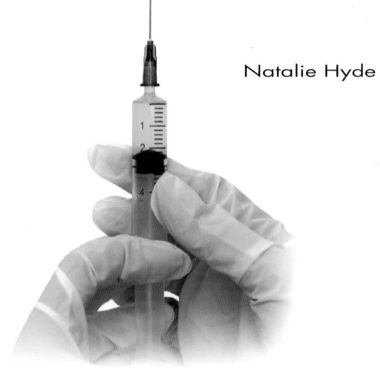

Natalie Hyde

Crabtree Publishing Company

www.crabtreebooks.com

SHAPING MODERN SCIENCE

Author: Natalie Hyde

Publishing plan research and development:
Sean Charlebois, Reagan Miller
Crabtree Publishing Company

Editors: Mary Lindeen, Adrianna Morganelli

Proofreaders: Gina Springer Shirley, Molly Aloian

Project coordinator: Kathy Middleton

Editorial services: Clarity Content Services

Production coordinator and prepress technician:
Katherine Berti

Print coordinator: Katherine Berti

Series consultant: Eric Walters

Cover design: Katherine Berti

Design: First Image

Photo research: Linda Tanaka

Photographs: cover/title page Shutterstock; p4 Sebastian Kaulitzki/
iStock; p5 NOAA; p6 Elena Schweitzer/Dreamstime.com; p7 top ively/
Shutterstock, Madlen/Shutterstock; p8 Copperplate engraving from: J. Ch.
Thiemen, Haus-, Feld-, Koch-, Kunst-, etc Buch (Nürnberg 1682)/public
domain/wiki; p9 Steven Wynn/iStock; p10 Philip Sigin-Lavdanski/iStock;
p11 top John licensed under the Creative Commons Attribution 2.0 Generic
license/wiki, Prokhorova Nadiia/Shutterstock; p12 Public domain/wiki; p13
Prof. Jos van den Broek licensed under the Creative Commons Attribution-
Share Alike 3.0 Unported license; p14 Juanmonino/iStock; p15 Mirek
Hejnicki/Dreamstime.com; p16 Edal Anton Lefterov licensed under the
Creative Commons Attribution-Share Alike 3.0 Unported license; p17
Portrait of Anthonie van Leeuwenhoek (1632-1723) currently in Naturalis,
National Museum of Natural History/public domain/wiki; p18 top
NOAA Public Library/public domain/wiki, From Scheme I. of his 1665
Micrographia. On permanent display in "The Evolution of the Microscope"
exhibit at the National Museum of Health and Medicine, in Washington,
DC/public domain/wiki; p19 left The cork described in "Micrographia" by
Robert Hooke/public domain/wiki, Public domain/wiki; p20 CDC/James
Hicks; p21 CDC/Dr. Fred Murphy and Sylvia Whitfield; p22 Pamela Moore/
iStock; p23 walterq/BigStock; p24 original in Musee d'Orsay Paris/public
domain/wiki; p25 top Lamiot licensed under the Creative Commons
Attribution 3.0 Unported license, Photo courtesy of Jacob Bourjaily; p26
LuisFico/BigStock; p27 top National Institutes of Health/USA; p28 CDC/
United States Department of Health and Human Services; p29 Henrik Jonsson/
iStock; p30 michal hrncir/iStock; p31, 32 CDC/Cynthia Goldsmith; p33
Sebastian Kaulitzki/iStock; p34 Dicdesign/BigStock; p35 CDC/Dr. E. Arum,
Dr. N. Jacobs; p36 scubabartek/BigStock; p37 top Henrik Larsson/
Shutterstock, Reuters; p38 top Peter Halasz licensed under the Creative
Commons Attribution-Share Alike 2.5 Generic, 2.0 Generic and 1.0 Generic
license, Nancy Nehring/iStock; p39 Mary Evans/Photo Researchers, Inc.;
p40 PD-USGov-HHS-CDC; p41 Brian Maudsley/iStock; pp42-43 Joseph R.
Schmitt/US Navy; p45 normanack licensed under the Creative Commons
Attribution 2.0 Generic license; p46 Magdalena Kucova/iStock; p47 top
Sailorr/Shutterstock, bitt24/Shutterstock; p48 Library of Congress; p49
Duncan Walker/iStock; p50-51 Library of Congress; p52 Alexander Raths/
iStock; p53 Volker Brinkmann licensed under the Creative Commons
Attribution 2.5 Generic license; pp54-55 Guntars Grebezs/iStock; p56 top
CDC/James Gathany, Nephron licensed under the Creative Commons
Attribution-Share Alike 3.0 Unported license; p57 LajosRepasi/iStock

Library and Archives Canada Cataloguing in Publication

Hyde, Natalie, 1963-
    What is germ theory? / Natalie Hyde.

(Shaping modern science)
Includes index.
Issued also in electronic format.
ISBN 978-0-7787-7201-9 (bound).–ISBN 978-0-7787-7208-8 (pbk.)

    1. Germ theory of disease–Juvenile literature. I. Title.
II. Series: Shaping modern science

RB153.H93 2011   j616.9'041   C2011-900180-2

Library of Congress Cataloging-in-Publication Data

Hyde, Natalie, 1963-
    What is germ theory? / Natalie Hyde.
        p. cm. -- (Shaping modern science)
    Includes index.
    ISBN 978-0-7787-7208-8 (pbk. : alk. paper) --
    ISBN 978-0-7787-7201-9 (reinforced library binding : alk. paper) -- ISBN
    978-1-4271-9530-2 (electronic (pdf))
    1. Germ theory of disease--Juvenile literature. I. Title. II. Series.

    RB153.H93 2011
    615'.37--dc22
                                            2010052631

Crabtree Publishing Company

www.crabtreebooks.com   1-800-387-7650

Printed in the U.S.A./102011/CG20110916

**Published in
Canada
Crabtree Publishing**
616 Welland Ave.
St. Catharines, ON
L2M 5V6

**Published in the
United States
Crabtree Publishing**
PMB 59051
350 Fifth Avenue, 59th Floor
New York, New York 10118

**Published in the
United Kingdom
Crabtree Publishing**
Maritime House
Basin Road North, Hove
BN41 1WR

**Published in
Australia
Crabtree Publishing**
386 Mt. Alexander Rd.
Ascot Vale (Melbourne)
VIC 3032

Contents

What Is Germ Theory?

There is a world around us that we cannot see; living organisms so small it takes powerful microscopes to see them. But being tiny hasn't stopped them from having a big effect on the way we live. These microscopic creatures called germs can keep us well or make us sick. They live everywhere, from high in the atmosphere to deep in the ocean. They can survive even in extreme temperatures. Germs also live in every type of plant and animal.

Some germs that live in our bodies actually help it work. Our **intestines** have special bacteria that help us digest our food. They change nutrients into a form that our bodies can easily absorb. Yogurt often contains these friendly bacteria.

Other germs can be very harmful. These **pathogens** can cause diseases or even death in plants and animals, including humans. Our bodies have a defense system in place to help stop bad germs from entering and causing damage. Our **immune system** protects our bodies by recognizing and attacking invaders.

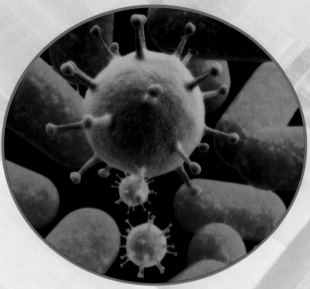

↑ Viruses and bacteria are everywhere!

Scientific Theory or Law?

In science, a *theory* is a well-tested set of ideas that explains how something occurs. For example, many kinds of evidence together support germ theory. A scientific *law* describes how something consistently happens under certain conditions. For example, the law of gravity describes how objects fall to Earth's surface.

An outer coating is the first way our immune system protects us. Some plants have a waxy surface that prevents germs from entering. Insects often have a shell or tough exoskeleton. Animals, like humans, have skin, fur, and hair to keep germs from having an easy entrance.

If pathogens do get inside, an organism will use a response like swelling or mucus to try to stop the invasion. If this doesn't work, the immune system sends special cells to attack the invaders. White blood cells can recognize bad germs, surround them, and kill them.

The immune system also has special memory cells. These cells can recognize parts of a pathogen called **antigens**. If the memory cells recognize antigens, they send out killer cells. The killer cells attach themselves to the invader and prevent it from spreading.

↑ Bacteria called thermophiles live in thermal vents like this one at the bottom of the ocean.

Fight Zone

An immune system that is too sensitive can cause damage to the body's own tissues. Certain allergies can trigger a severe reaction. For some people, bee stings can make their throats swell and put them in real danger. Other immune systems are too slow to react or don't react at all. This allows germs to grow and spread rapidly. AIDS is a virus that damages the immune system, making the body vulnerable to disease.

Kinds of Germs

Germs fall into four main groups: bacteria, viruses, fungi, and protozoa. Bacteria are one-celled organisms. They get nutrients from their environments. Sometimes that environment is the human body. When bacteria grow and multiply they can cause infections such as strep throat, cavities, and **pneumonia**.

Viruses cannot survive for long on their own. They need a host in order to reproduce. Once inside a cell they change the cell's instructions, or DNA, and attack the plant or animal from within. Viruses cause diseases such as influenza, colds, and chicken pox.

Fungi are multi-celled organisms that cannot manufacture their own food. They get their nutrients from a host organism. Tiny fungi like **yeasts** and molds can cause problems in humans. Athlete's foot is a rash caused by an **infectious** fungus that likes warm, moist places such as public showers or locker rooms.

Protozoa are single-celled organisms that live in damp places. Once inside animals, they can cause problems such as diarrhea or nausea. They can also cause diseases such as malaria.

←When we feel sick it is because germs have attacked our bodies.

Quick fact

Researchers use a set of ideas called a *theory* to explain why things happen in nature. Scientific theories are tested using experiments. Failed experiments teach scientists that their theories need to be improved or changed.

In ancient times, people tried to understand what caused sickness. They didn't have microscopes or laboratories to study the human body. They could only watch what was happening and try to understand it.

Many people believed in **spontaneous regeneration**. This was the idea that living things could come from nonliving materials. For example, blisters from chicken pox seemed to come out of nowhere. These, like many diseases, were blamed on bad air or evil spirits.

Sometimes healers accidentally found cures that worked. Wounds that were covered in honey seemed to heal faster than other wounds. The healers didn't know that honey has properties that prevent bacteria from growing. Healers used honey because bees were thought to be pure and honey was the drink of the gods.

Your tongue is germ–free only when it's pink. If it is white, it has a thin layer of bacteria on it.

Historical Footnote

When scientists test and observe the same reaction happening over and over again, they can state a scientific law. Sir Isaac Newton, English mathematician and physicist (1642-1727), studied the motion of the planets around the Sun. From his observations he developed a law about gravity.

Curious Cookbook

The theory of spontaneous regeneration led to some strange recipes. To make mice, women were told to put a dirty cloth in wheat for 21 days. If they buried a bull's head in the ground with the horns sticking out, after one month they would have bees.

CHAPTER ONE

A History of Germs

Before germs were discovered, people believed that diseases were a punishment for sins and crimes. If a whole village got sick, they thought it was the work of demons or evil spirits. Others thought that their enemies made them sick by using magic.

Healers used spells, charms, and even threats as cures. They would ask the gods to send away the evil spirits causing the sickness. Healers might also use bad-tasting and smelly potions to make the evil spirits want to leave a patient's body.

Some people wore charms around their necks or carried them in a pouch to keep away evil spirits. Special stones, carvings, or animal teeth and bones were thought to be powerful protection for the person wearing them.

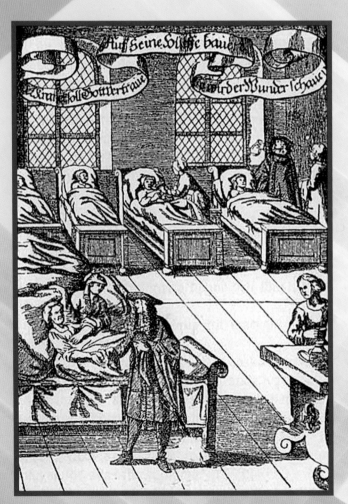

←In earlier times, hospitals were often places where diseases were spread through unclean methods and overcrowding.

Some healers would drill a hole in the back of a patient's skull to release an evil spirit. **Archaeologists** around the world have found old skulls with holes drilled in them. This is how they know that many ancient healers used this treatment, called trepanning.

Other healers believed that people got sick because their blood stayed in one place and got stale. **Bloodletting** was a way to get rid of these unhealthy areas in the body. A healer would make a small cut in the patient's body to let the blood out. Other early doctors used leeches. Millions of leeches were used every year for bloodletting.

Fevers and headaches were common reasons for bloodletting. It was also used to treat acne, asthma, cancer, diabetes, insanity, leprosy, strokes, and many other diseases.

→Potions were usually made with herbs, plants, bark, roots, and seeds. Old potion recipes were handed down from generation to generation.

Quick fact

Leeches are still used in medicine today but not for bloodletting. They are used to help restore circulation after reattaching limbs.

Shave and a Cut?

In the 1100s, physicians stopped performing bloodletting and other surgeries. Barbers took over this work and also did lancings and **amputations**. The red-and-white striped barber's pole still seen today was the sign used to identify a barber-surgeon and to let the public know of their services.

The Father of Medicine

Ideas about the cause of sickness started to change with a physician named Hippocrates. He was born in 460 B.C. in Kos, Greece. He didn't believe that evil spirits invaded the body or that illnesses were **supernatural**.

Hippocrates believed that disease had physical and natural causes. He thought that a healthy body had a balance of four fluids, called humors. Too much or too little of any one fluid would make a person ill.

He also believed in observing a patient and taking careful notes. Hippocrates trained his students to do this. They took careful measurements of a patient's **symptoms**, including pulse, skin color, movements, and temperature. He thought it would be useful for future doctors to be able to refer to these notes.

↑ *Hippocrates learned medicine from his father and grandfather. He in turn taught his two sons and son-in-law.*

Quick fact

Because he changed the way people thought about disease and healing, Hippocrates is known as the "Father of Medicine."

"Cure sometimes, treat often, comfort always."

—Hippocrates, 460 B.C.–ca. 370 B.C.

Hippocrates thought the body should be treated as a whole system and not just a series of parts. He also believed that the body had the power to heal itself as long as the four humors were in balance.

His treatments were very gentle. They had more to do with keeping the patient comfortable and resting than actually giving any medicine. He insisted on very clean, sterile surroundings. He also said that doctors should be calm, honest, and neat. They even had to cut their fingernails. This was very different from ancient healers, who would never think to wash their hands no matter how dirty they were. Without knowing about germs, Hippocrates had come up with one of the most important rules for preventing disease.

↑Hippocrates has had many things named after him, including symptoms of diseases, special bandages, hospitals, and even a crater on the moon.

I Swear

The Hippocratic Oath was a sworn statement made by students studying medicine under Hippocrates. It reminds doctors to first do no harm to their patients, to share their knowledge, and to protect the privacy of patients. Many medical schools today use a modern version of this oath for graduating students.

Swamps and Bad Air

Once people accepted the idea that sickness did not come from evil spirits, they began to look for other causes. Marcus Varro was a Roman born in 116 B.C. He thought that tiny life forms might cause illness.

During his life, Varro wrote more than 620 books. In one of them, he warned people to stay away from swamps and marshes. He wrote that such areas "breed certain minute creatures which cannot be seen by the eyes, but which float in the air and enter the body through the mouth and nose and cause serious diseases."

Varro said that the sun and good air circulation would stop these tiny creatures from multiplying. He thought that a wind would blow them away and they would die of dryness.

Varro's ideas were mostly ignored. It wasn't until hundreds of years later that scientists realized how close he had come to the truth about germs and disease.

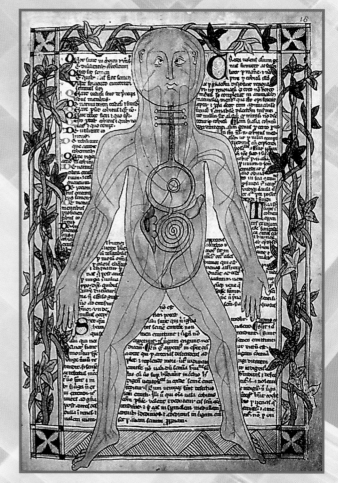

↑ This thirteenth-century drawing shows the veins.

Quick fact

Even though Roman surgeons did not know about germ theory, medical schools advised them to boil their **surgical** tools and bowls before starting an operation.

In the Middle Ages, people believed that "bad air" called miasma brought diseases. They identified this bad air by its terrible smell, which they thought came from floating bits of rotting material.

People began avoiding areas with stale, polluted water. Walking in beautifully smelling gardens and "taking the air" at the seaside was how they thought they could avoid or even cure sickness.

Scientists had still not discovered germs were the real cause of illnesses. However, improvements in **sanitation** to get rid of polluted water and air did help stop the spread of some diseases.

↑In the Middle Ages, doctors began to perform autopsies and study the human body.

"For when the morning breezes blow toward the town at sunrise, if they bring with them mist from marshes and, mingled with the mist, the poisonous breath of creatures of the marshes to be wafted into the bodies of the inhabitants, they will make the site unhealthy."

—Vitruvius, Roman writer and architect, first century B.C.

The Big Cover-up

In Italy, doctors who visited **plague** victims wore a "plague mask." It had a long beak that the doctors stuffed with spices to protect them from the miasma, which they thought carried the disease.

Poisons and Spores

↑*Long ago, medicine was made for each person individually, depending on the illness of the patient and the doctor's favorite recipe.*

Phillip von Hohenheim, also known as Paracelsus, was a Swiss doctor born in 1493. He also thought sickness had a natural cause. He wasn't sure that bad air was to blame, though. He believed that toxins in food and from space could poison the body and make it sick.

Even though he did not know **anatomy**, Paracelsus tried using chemicals and minerals as medicine. He used mercury to cure certain diseases.

He also pointed out the benefits of mineral water. He even tried to make it himself.

Paracelsus thought that any substance could be helpful or harmful, depending on how much was taken. He thought that even water, which is necessary for the body, could be deadly if there was too much. It was his goal in life to find a cure for every disease.

Cholera Epidemic, India, 1816

Because people had the wrong idea about where diseases came from and how they were spread, a disease could spread rapidly. Cholera is caused by bacteria in the intestines. The cholera **epidemic** that started in India spread as far west as Africa and east to Japan. More than 15 million people died.

Girolamo Fracastoro was a doctor born in 1478 in Verona, Italy. Even though the microscope had not been invented and he had never seen a germ, Fracastoro believed that tiny **spores** carried the seeds of disease.

Fracastoro believed these small particles could multiply quickly. He also thought they could be spread on infected cloth or through the air. Once a person touched infected cloth or breathed infected air, they could also become infected.

↑Early laboratories were often very primitive. Scientists had only basic equipment and chemicals to use for experiments.

Francastoro was close to discovering germ theory. However, most people ignored his ideas. Bad air was something people could smell themselves. It was impossible to prove the existence of tiny invisible spores.

Quick fact

Because of his work in alchemy, Paracelsus was the first person to use chemistry to help cure diseases. Alchemy is the art of trying to turn common metals into gold and silver.

CHAPTER TWO

Ideas and Experiments

With the invention of the microscope, scientists could finally get a look at the tiny life forms they had wondered about for years.

Eyeglass makers in the Netherlands were the first to put two lenses together to make a simple microscope. A Dutch scientist named Antonie van Leeuwenhoek made improvements to it. He then saw a world that had been too small to be seen.

Leeuwenhoek began by looking at parts of bees. As he made smaller and smaller lenses, he could magnify their mouthparts and stingers more and more. He also looked at the microscopic life forms that lived in water.

↑ *The compound microscope has changed very little since it was invented in 1590.*

He was amazed to see single-cell organisms, the first germs seen by anyone. At last there was proof that tiny life forms existed. He studied bacteria that live in the human mouth and one-celled organisms called **protists**.

He wrote of his discoveries and sent the work to the Royal Society of London. At first they didn't believe him. No one had ever seen microorganisms before. They suggested that Leeuwenhoek wasn't clear on what he was seeing or maybe was not right in his mind. Leeuwenhoek told them to send a group of experts to come study his findings. After seeing for themselves, the Society finally agreed that microorganisms exist.

Quick fact

The Royal Society of London for the Improvement of Natural Knowledge is a group devoted to improving our understanding of the world. The Society has funded research and experiments for more than 450 years.

←Antonie van Leeuwenhoek is known as the "Father of Microbiology."

Night Job

Leeuwenhoek wanted to keep his lens-making process a secret. He pretended he spent hours and hours at night grinding glass into the right shape. In fact, he used soda lime glass heated over a hot flame to make a glass ball. He was afraid that if microscopes became common items, his name would be forgotten.

Hooke and Redi

Robert Hooke was a scientific genius. This English scientist designed new machines, studied springs and **elasticity**, learned to measure the distance between stars, and built clocks.

He also improved the microscope even further by giving it a source of light. He was able to study the smallest parts of insects and draw them clearly. He was also able to see the **microbes** that Leeuwenhoek described.

Under the microscope, Hooke also studied plants. He thought that the tiny sections that made up cork looked a little like monks' living quarters in a monastery. He named these tiny building blocks

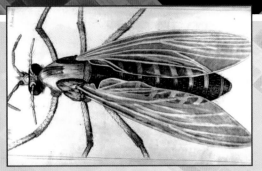

↑Hooke used his microscope to make detailed drawings, such as this one of a gnat.

"cells" after the monks' rooms. This name was then used to describe the smallest parts of any living thing.

The discovery of tiny living things all around them made some scientists wonder if animals really came from nonliving things. The idea of spontaneous regeneration had been around for centuries. Now scientists began to ask if the tiny life seen in microscopes could better explain the source of *all* life.

↓Hooke used a candle to provide a light source for the microscope.

Quick fact

Robert Hooke's book *Micrographia*, published in 1665, includes his drawings of a fly's eye, a louse, and plant cells. It can be viewed online.

Francesco Redi was an Italian biologist and physician. He suspected that flies that seemed to come from meat actually came from eggs on the meat. What if the eggs were too small to be seen?

He came up with an experiment. He put pieces of meat inside several jars. Half he sealed with a lid, half he left open. **Maggots** appeared only on the meat in the open jars.

To prove that air, good or bad, had nothing to do with it, Redi did a second experiment. Half the jars were covered with a fine material that let in air but not insects. The other jars were uncovered. Again, maggots only appeared on the meat in the uncovered jars.

↓*Micrographia was published in 1665 and was a scientific best-seller.*

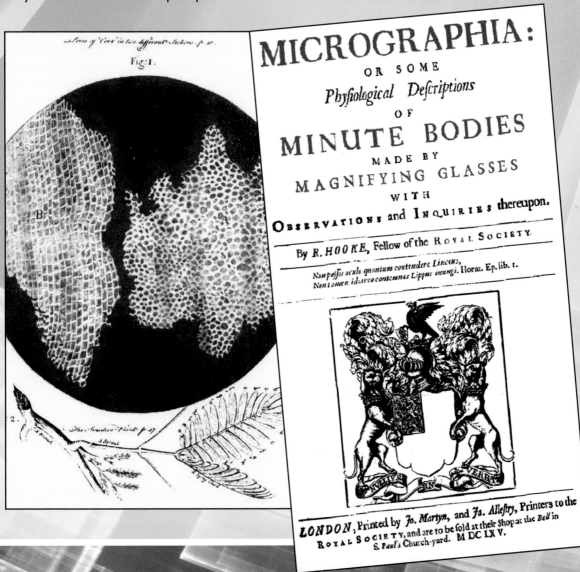

Understanding Germs and Disease

Once people understood that illness was not caused by evil spirits, they looked for new ways to protect themselves. Charms would not stop germs from entering their bodies.

Early physicians noticed that people who had survived one attack of a disease, even a mild one, almost never suffered from that disease again. This was especially true of the deadly smallpox virus. India and China seem to be the first countries to use this information to try to stop the spread of disease. Records in medical texts from the eighth century describe **inoculating** against smallpox.

↑ *The smallpox rash usually starts on the forehead and can spread to the whole body in 24 to 36 hours.*

Historical Footnote

Because of vaccination programs, in December 1979, smallpox became the first human infectious disease to have been wiped out.

There seemed to be two types of the disease: a mild one, and another severe and often deadly one. Doctors would take scabs from a minor case and put them on a wad of cotton. Then they would place the cotton in the nose of a healthy person. The healthy person would develop a mild case of smallpox. But they would usually recover, and they would be protected from the more serious type.

Did You Know?

The earliest evidence of smallpox was on a pharaoh in Egypt. Ramses V had the familiar rash on his **mummified** body.

"I hope that some day the practice of producing cowpox in human beings will spread over the world—when that day comes, there will be no more smallpox."

—Edward Jenner (1749–1823)

More than half of the children who got smallpox died from it. Their immune systems were not strong enough to fight the virus. The first people to ask for inoculations were often nobles or royalty. They wanted to protect their children.

The idea of inoculating spread to Europe and then to America. In 1796, Edward Jenner discovered that the cowpox virus rarely caused death in humans but would protect them against smallpox. Inoculating people using the cowpox virus was much safer. Soon using smallpox scabs was banned.

↓An electron micrograph is a photograph taken through a microscope. This one shows the smallpox virus.

WARNING!

Smallpox was an infectious disease caused by the variola virus. It caused a rash of raised bumps and blisters and affected the internal organs. One third of all people who got smallpox died, about 400,000 people per year in the 1800s. A third of those who survived became blind from the disease.

CHAPTER THREE

Germ Theory Takes Shape

With the success of vaccinations against smallpox, some scientists began to make connections between microorganisms and disease. Others kept their old ideas.

One doctor, Ignaz Semmelweis, tried to convince others that tiny poisonous particles could exist on doctors' hands. He came to believe this after working at a hospital during the 1840s.

Childbed fever killed many women after they gave birth. Semmelweis noticed fewer deaths from this illness when his medical students washed their hands before examining the patients.

Most medical students had come from studying dead bodies before beginning their hospital work. He believed dead bodies **contaminated** the students' hands with harmful microscopic particles.

Almost no women died from childbed fever when the staff washed their hands before touching patients. But other doctors did not believe Semmelweis. The other doctors still believed the deaths were caused by miasma.

Semmelweis became very angry that people didn't believe him. He was eventually put in an insane asylum, where he died two weeks later. Hospital staff stopped washing their hands, and the death rate rose again.

↓ Humans have about 200 million bacteria on their hands. Imagine how many germs dirty hands have!

Only a few years later, in 1854, there was a cholera outbreak in London, England. Another physician, John Snow, marked the locations of cholera victims on a map of London. He noticed that they were all a short distance from one certain water pump. Contaminated water was seeping into the well from a cesspit. It was near where a child had been sick with cholera.

Snow had local officials take off the handle of the pump so it could not be used. Fewer people got sick. This convinced Snow that something in the water was spreading the disease.

→ *John Snow was one of the first doctors to use ether and chloroform to make patients unconscious during surgery. This process became standard in medical textbooks.*

After the outbreak, officials replaced the pump handle. They rejected Snow's theory. Once again, people went back to old ideas even when there was proof that a new idea had been on the right track.

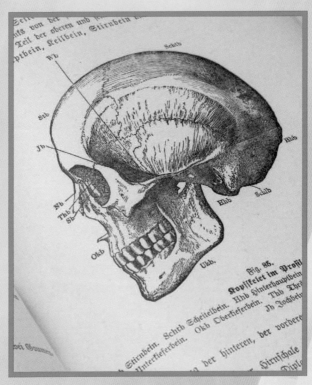

It Was the Pits!

A cesspit was a large hole dug in the ground under houses. Human waste collected in the pit caused terrible odors to seep up through the floors. People still blamed diseases, sudden deaths, and plagues on the air and didn't realize dangerous microorganisms were **leeching** from their cesspits into their wells.

Learning to Kill Germs

↑ *Louis Pasteur was a professor of chemistry at the University of Strasbourg, in Alsace, France.*

French chemist Louis Pasteur finally proved that the theories of miasma and spontaneous regeneration were wrong.

In 1863, Pasteur was asked to find out why some wine would spoil and taste bitter. Using his microscope, Pasteur saw the microorganism yeast in the liquid. Some scientists believed its growth in the wine was proof of spontaneous regeneration.

Pasteur wanted to prove them wrong. He set up an experiment using broth similar to Redi's meat experiment. The yeast was only in jars that were uncovered. Scientists finally had to agree that tiny organisms were alive in the air.

Pasteur discovered that microorganisms caused wine, milk, and meat to spoil. He learned that these germs could be killed with heat. This also finally convinced doctors to sterilize their instruments before surgery to kill any germs living on them.

"Where observation is concerned, chance favors only the prepared mind."

—Louis Pasteur, 1854

Did You Know?

The process of using heat to kill harmful bacteria in food was named after Louis Pasteur. We still use "pasteurization" today to keep milk fresh.

↑ The image of Louis Pasteur looks out from the grounds of the Institut Pasteur de Lille, a research center in France.

Quick fact

Pasteur would let nothing stop his work. When the university would not supply a laboratory, he used a tiny workspace under some stairs that he could only reach by crawling on his hands and knees.

Pasteur wanted to use science to help business and industry. Silkworms spin a very thin, soft thread that is woven to make silk fabric. Something was killing silkworms. Pasteur was able to study the microorganism that was attacking the worms. Then he could find ways to control its spread.

He also wanted to help farmers whose animals died from disease. He developed vaccines to prevent **anthrax** in animals and to control the deadly rabies disease in animals and humans.

Because of Pasteur's work, other scientists finally began to give up their old theories. Ideas about miasma and spontaneous regeneration were replaced with the theory of microorganisms, or germ theory.

← In 1960, Pasteur was featured on the 5 franc note. The picture also includes a statue of a 15-year-old boy Pasteur saved from rabies, some of the animals Pasteur used in his experiments, and equipment from his lab.

Two Important Discoveries

As more doctors and scientists accepted the fact that germs were everywhere, it changed the way they handled patients, surgeries, and disease.

Joseph Lister, born in 1827, was a British surgeon who made more improvements to the microscope. He studied the germs that Pasteur had written about. He was interested in Pasteur's ideas about sterilizing surgical instruments.

↑Medical instruments can be sterilized using heat, chemicals, or pressure.

Many of Lister's patients survived surgery but died from infections afterward. He couldn't use heat to kill the germs in wounds. He had to come up with another way.

Lister found that fewer patients died when he used **carbolic acid** to clean their wounds. He also switched from stitches made with silk thread to using catgut soaked in carbolic acid. Lister was practicing **antisepsis**, or preventing the spread of germs with chemicals.

Like Semmelweis, Lister also made surgeons wash their hands before touching patients. This time doctors listened.

Quick fact

Listerine, a brand of mouthwash, is named after Joseph Lister.

With the invention of the microscope and the discovery of microorganisms, scientists and doctors were now working to cure diseases. They wanted to keep people safe and healthy. They also wanted to stop diseases in animals.

Robert Koch was a German doctor who became the director of the Institute for Infectious Diseases in 1891. The first disease he studied was anthrax in cattle. The harmful bacteria had been found, but not a cure.

Koch studied the anthrax germ. As part of his work, he came up with useful methods for **isolating** and growing bacteria. His guidelines helped scientists identify many pathogens over the next ten years. These included tuberculosis, cholera, typhoid fever, and diphtheria.

↑Robert Koch received the Nobel Prize in Medicine, in 1905, for his work with tuberculosis.

The Koch Postulates

Robert Koch's process for isolating and growing bacteria became known as the Koch Postulates. According to these rules, in order to prove that an organism is the cause of a disease:

- it must be present in every victim of the disease;
- it must be prepared and maintained in a pure culture;
- the culture must be able to produce the original infection;
- it can be taken from a new victim and cultured again.

↑A "pure culture" refers to bacteria growing in a laboratory dish with no other organisms present.

CHAPTER FOUR

What Are Viruses?

Viruses are one type of germ. Because they are so small, they were not discovered as quickly as bacteria.

The first germs that scientists were able to see in microscopes were bacteria. They learned that bacteria caused many diseases in animals and humans. But for some of the diseases scientists were studying, they couldn't find any bacteria.

Scientists developed a filter so fine that it could strain out even the tiniest bacteria. They were confused then when infections were still sometimes found even though all bacteria had been strained out. They realized that there must be something even smaller that could cause disease.

German chemist Adolf Mayer was studying the tobacco **mosaic** disease in plants. He could infect a healthy tobacco plant by using the juice of a diseased one. He thought tiny bacteria created poisons that spread the disease.

Russian biologist Dmitri Ivanovsky found the same thing. But he believed the disease was caused by some other very tiny living thing. He didn't know it, but he had just discovered the world's first virus.

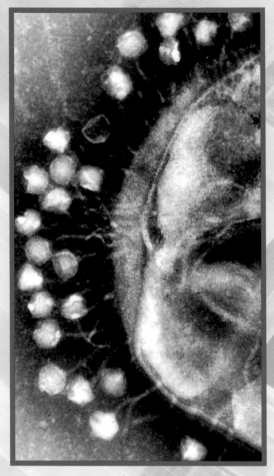

↑ Viruses attack a bacterium.

Historical Footnote

The first person to name this new pathogen a "virus" was Dutch microbiologist Marinus Beijerinck.

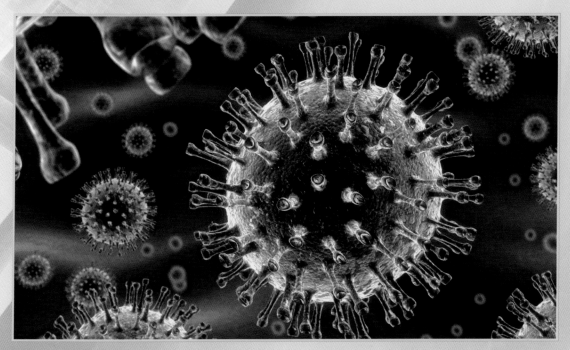

↑*This is an HIV virus as seen through a microscope.*

Scientists knew that they needed an even stronger microscope if they ever hoped to see this new germ called a virus. Even the most powerful lenses could only magnify objects up to 2,000 times their original size.

In 1931, a new type of microscope was invented. Instead of using light, it used a beam of electrons. Instead of a glass lens, it used a magnetic field. This allowed scientists to magnify objects many times more than the original **optical** microscope could. The first electron microscopes were able to reach magnifications of 30,000 times the original size.

Electron microscopes have some disadvantages. Because they bounce beams off the surface of objects, certain materials do not produce a good picture. For example, insects may need to be coated with a metal such as gold in order to produce a clear picture. However, the coating materials can damage some delicate samples.

Quick fact

The newest electron microscopes can reach magnifications of up to 2,000,000 times!

Viruses and Disease

Scientists were hard at work trying to figure out exactly what viruses were. How were they different from bacteria? They knew that viruses could not be grown in laboratory dishes like bacteria. They needed a new way to isolate and study this new life form.

Quick fact

The tobacco mosaic virus was the first virus ever identified.

Wendell Stanley was an American chemist. He was working on the tobacco mosaic virus. He was able to **crystallize** the virus into thin rod-like crystals. Now he could better study its structure.

Stanley was also able to prove that even after crystallization, the virus was still infectious. Many scientists doubted this. They thought viruses were like bacteria, which could not exist as crystals.

Stanley fought hard to convince other scientists that viruses could be in a pure form, and that once they were crystallized, they could be studied and tested with chemicals.

Healthy Plants, Healthy People

The tobacco mosaic virus not only infects tobacco plants but also other plants, such as tomatoes, peppers, and cucumbers. Scientists worked on this virus because controlling this disease would help the food supplies of many countries.

Stanley wanted to use his knowledge to understand human viruses. He was very interested in creating vaccines for infections like influenza and **polio**.

The first vaccine ever made was used against smallpox. At first doctors injected people with a live but weak smallpox virus. Later they used the cowpox virus. But it can be dangerous to give a live form of the disease to some people. Children or people with weak immune systems might still get sick from the disease.

So scientists looked for a better way. They tried treating some viruses with chemicals. The virus would still have the same structure, but it couldn't reproduce and cause disease. This way, a person's body would mark these germs as invaders and fight them. Rabies and influenza vaccines use this kind of inactivated virus.

For other diseases, a virus is changed, or mutated. It is still alive when injected, but it cannot reproduce quickly. It is then easily attacked by our immune systems. Many of the vaccines we have today, such as those for measles and mumps, use mutated, or **attenuated**, viruses.

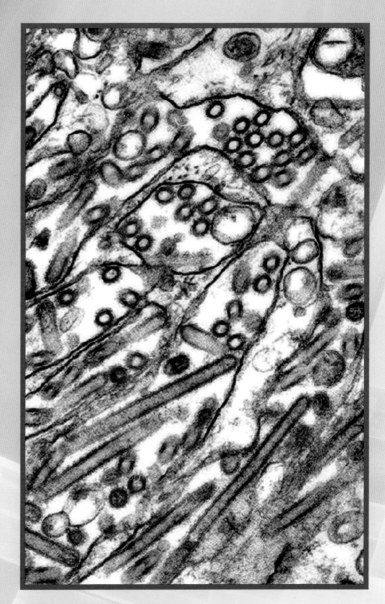

→ Viruses exist in many shapes and sizes.

How Viruses Live

Unlike bacteria, viruses are not able to reproduce on their own. They must infect a host cell and use that cell's energy. Viruses have three main parts: **genetic** instructions, a coating of protein that protects this information, and sometimes a layer of fat outside the protein coat.

Also unlike bacteria, viruses have no parts to help them move. They have to rely on outside forces to help them find their host cells. Traveling on water, wind, and insects are some of the ways viruses get around.

Once a virus finds a host cell in a victim, it attaches to the cell wall. Then it injects its own genetic information into the host cell. This allows the virus to take over and use the cell's energy to reproduce.

↑A virus invades a cell wall.

Quick fact

Some viruses attack other germs such as bacteria. This type of virus is called a bacteriophage.

Viruses are the most abundant **parasites** on Earth. They infect humans, animals, plants, and bacteria.

Sometimes viruses don't cause any damage to a host cell. These are called latent, or inactive, viruses. A latent virus can lay **dormant** for months or years.

Other viruses destroy host cells. Once the newly formed virus has reproduced, it may burst out of a cell and seek new host cells. Other viruses turn off the instructions in a host cell that control how often it divides. This can make cells multiply without stopping, creating **tumors**.

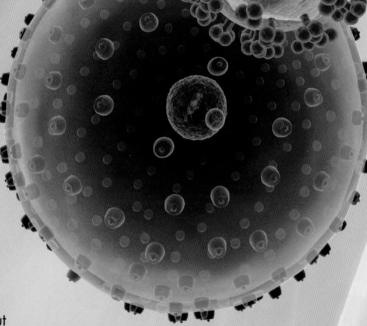

↑ *Viruses use spikes to attach themselves to a host cell.*

The Quick-change Artist: Influenza

One of the reasons influenza has been so hard to control is because the virus is a master of disguise. It mutates very easily, making it hard for the immune system to identify and kill it. Vaccines have to target large groups of many types of the disease because each year new influenza strains develop.

Studying Viruses

As far as we know, viruses have been around for as long as there has been life on our planet. However, scientists have had a hard time trying to discover where viruses came from.

There is no fossil record of viruses. Also, the oldest viruses we can examine are only about 100 years old. Viruses also change, or mutate, very quickly. Researchers have tried to look at modern viruses and compare related groups. They look for patterns of change and try to work backward to find the original virus.

Some scientists believe viruses are the leftover parts of tiny organisms. Others think they are mutated cells that lost their ability to reproduce without a host. Still others think they came from the same chemical "soup" that started all life on the planet.

↑A virus grows in a cell culture dish.

Yellow Fever Is Not Afraid to Change

Yellow fever virus started in central Africa where it infected certain monkeys. Mosquitoes that bit the monkeys would then carry the virus, which had adapted to live in both creatures. The mosquitoes would then infect other animals, including humans. Once again, the virus was able to adapt to new hosts. A vaccine now exists to prevent this serious and deadly disease.

"...you have to worry about something else, too, because somehow, somewhere, the virus is coming from a place that we haven't yet identified."

—Dr. Anthony Fauci (1940–)

Each time a virus moves into a new host cell, the virus finds a way to copy itself. This allows the virus to spread. Sometimes it makes mistakes when it copies itself, and these mistakes in turn change the virus. These changes can create a stronger or weaker virus.

Some changes mean viruses can fit a new type of host. This is how some diseases jump from animals to humans. These new-to-human viruses are especially dangerous because our bodies have not had a chance to build an immunity to them.

Another problem for scientists and doctors are drug-resistant viruses and bacteria. These germs have changed so much that they can survive in chemicals meant to kill them. This means that scientists have to keep inventing new and stronger drugs to fight disease.

↑Drug-resistant viruses can cause a disease to come back quicker and stronger.

Did You Know?

H5N1 is called bird flu because scientists have traced its beginnings to bird populations in southeast Asia. It spread to humans and became a serious problem. Sixty percent of people who became infected died. Scientists worry that the virus will mutate again and become a deadly **pandemic**.

CHAPTER FIVE

Fighting Back!

Before people knew about germs, sickness seemed to come out of nowhere and spread quickly. Many people died of diseases not knowing that they were spreading the germs on their clothing and hands and in their food.

Scientists found it difficult to convince doctors that they should wash their hands between patients. Doctors were insulted when people suggested their hands could be dirty. They thought they were too smart and important to cause the diseases they were trying to cure. As a result, when an epidemic would hit, people were helpless. All they could do was sit back and wait for it to pass. They would pray and even make sacrifices to the gods to spare their families. Knowing that entire families or villages could be wiped out by a disease was just a part of life.

The Black Death

The bubonic plague was one of the deadliest diseases in history. It spread quickly out of central Asia in every direction, into Africa and all through Europe. Between 1347 and 1351, over 25 million people died from it. Infected sailors unknowingly brought it to new areas when their ships docked. The disease was spread by infected rats. The rats would hide aboard ships, and once on land would be bitten by fleas that would then bite humans. Most people believed the "black death" was God's punishment for their sins.

The Bite in the Night

The germs that cause malaria and yellow fever are both carried by mosquitoes. By spraying ponds and pools where mosquitoes breed, the spread of these diseases can be reduced before they reach humans.

Most people didn't believe in germs until they could see them. Change only came once the microscope gave proof of these once invisible creatures. People then had to think differently about disease, medicine, and cleanliness.

Doctors and scientists then realized that disease did not come from **mystical** forces, miasmas, or demons. The source of disease was something that could be seen, tested, and hopefully controlled. This allowed scientists to spend their time finding cures for some of the world's most serious diseases. Vaccines offered some protection, but they did not work for everyone. Some people were too weak to fight off even a mild case of a disease. Scientists hoped to find new ways to slow or stop illnesses by studying the life cycle of the germs that caused them.

→ *People in Japan have made face masks fashionable. For years the Japanese have been preventing the spread of disease by wearing cloth masks that cover the nose and mouth. By covering their faces, they know they can stop germs from getting into their bodies and avoid spreading their own germs if they get sick.*

Fleming's Accidental Discovery

The first big breakthrough in new germ-fighting medication happened by accident. Alexander Fleming had left some bacteria growing on culture plates when he went away on vacation. When he came back, one of the plates had mold on it that seemed to be killing the bacteria. He took a closer look and saw that the mold ate away at the bacteria. The Scottish doctor wondered if this mold could be a cure for the disease caused by that bacteria.

↑ *This penicillium has been stained purple so it can be studied more closely.*

Battling Bacteria

Staphylococcus means "bunch of grapes" in Greek. And that is exactly what this bacteria looks like under a microscope. These little round germs tend to cluster together in groups. *Staphylococcus* can cause many types of infection in humans and other animals. This is the kind of bacteria Fleming had been growing on his culture plates. It was very exciting when he thought he might have found a way to fight such a harmful germ.

There were problems with growing the mold, however. Fleming found that the mold, which he named *Penicillium notatum*, didn't stay active for long. He needed to find out how the mold killed bacteria. It turned out there was a chemical substance in the mold that killed bacteria. He called this substance penicillin. Fleming did not have a biochemist on his staff, so he asked others to help him make something useful out of his accidental discovery.

↓ *Penicillium mold, shown here, can also be used to make blue cheese.*

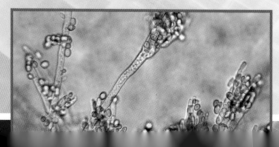

Fleming continued to grow the original mold for 12 years. He asked every chemist he knew to help him make penicillin.

Howard Florey and Ernst Chain found new ways to isolate penicillin. They wanted to create enough of it to use in tests. Eventually, factories were built to make penicillin on a large scale.

Doctors began testing penicillin on humans in 1942. They were amazed to see quick results from this new **antibacterial** drug. Serious infections such as gangrene and pneumonia were now treatable. Bacteria that infected wounds could be stopped. Doctors would not need to perform as many amputations.

↑Fleming works in his laboratory.

"When I woke up just after dawn on September 28, 1928, I certainly didn't plan to revolutionize all medicine by discovering the world's first antibiotic, or bacteria killer, but I suppose that was exactly what I did."

—Alexander Fleming

Quick fact

Alexander Fleming, Howard Florey, and Ernst Chain shared the Nobel Prize in 1945 for their work with penicillin.

Using Antibiotics to Fight Disease

Fleming's discovery of penicillin was the beginning of modern antibiotics. Scientists began to create new drugs to fight even the most stubborn infections. This saved the lives of millions of people.

Scientists used dyes to create a chemical that attached itself to bacteria but not healthy tissue. This antibiotic worked well against infections such as childbed fever and blood infections.

Different antibiotics work in different ways. Some break through the cell wall of the bacteria, killing it. Others mess up the way the bacteria grow or reproduce. Still others stop the germs from making the energy they need to survive.

↑ Most antibiotics try to interrupt how bacteria, such as this one that causes childbed fever, function or grow.

Did You Know?

Antibiotics can be given to patients in different ways. They can be swallowed in pills or liquid and then absorbed into the body. They can be used on the outside of the body, such as ear or eye drops, or as a lotion or cream. For infections that are spread throughout the body or are otherwise very serious, antibiotics can be injected directly into the blood stream.

If too little penicillin was used or it was used for too short a time, bacteria would develop a **resistance** to it. The bacteria would create its own way to fight the penicillin. Fleming warned doctors not to give penicillin without being sure of the type of infection.

Sometimes hospitals used a low dose of antibiotics to prevent infections. This led to new types of bacteria resistant to antibiotics. Other times doctors used antibiotics to treat colds or influenza. These are caused by viruses. Antibiotics only kill bacteria, not viruses. Each time these drugs are used incorrectly, bacteria develop their own ways to resist the drugs.

Resistant germs are sometimes called superbugs. Stronger drugs have to be invented to kill these stronger bacteria. Researchers worry that this may allow diseases that have almost been wiped out to start coming back.

Quick fact

An antibiotic is any substance that kills or slows the growth of bacteria.

↓Bacteria clump together to form colonies to attack cells.

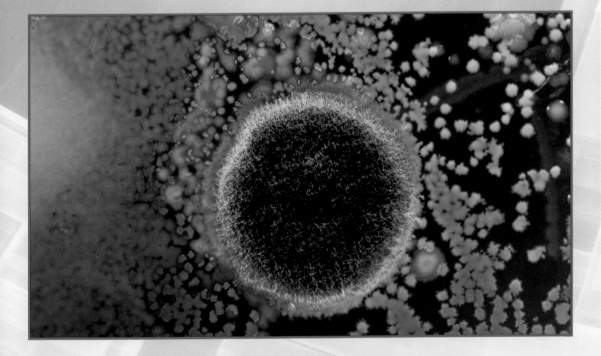

Using Antivirals to Fight Disease

To help fight viruses, researchers have created **antiviral** drugs. Just like antibiotics, different antivirals treat different viral infections. Unlike most antibiotics, antiviral drugs do not kill their targets. Antivirals can only slow the growth and reproduction of a virus. Because it uses a host cell, it is very hard to kill a virus without destroying its host cell, too.

Most antivirals created so far fight infections such as HIV, herpes, and hepatitis. These are serious infections that kill thousands of people every year. At first scientists would infect cells with a virus and then try different chemicals to see which ones slowed the virus. This was not a very useful way to find good treatments. Researchers learned how some viruses lived and reproduced. This gave scientists better ideas for stopping them.

Some medications are only for use on the outside of the body. Certain chemicals or herbal oils can turn off or destroy viruses. This is a good way to stop viruses before they enter the body and find host cells.

Inside the body, antiviral drugs identify a part of a virus, or the target. Some drugs stop a virus from attaching to a host cell. Others produce chemicals that make it hard for a virus to enter a host cell. Still others stop a virus from reproducing once it's inside a host cell. Another type of drug helps the body's immune system fight harder. These drugs help the body attack the germs.

Just like bacteria, viruses can develop resistance to drugs. This can happen quickly because viruses can mutate each time they reproduce. Sometimes two or more drugs are used at the same time to overcome drug resistance.

↓ *Thanks to vaccinations, the last case of smallpox was in 1977. Polio is also close to being wiped out.*

CHAPTER SIX

The Work of Germs

Once scientists were able to look in a microscope and see germs, they learned something astonishing: germs are everywhere!

They are on and in everything on Earth: plants, animals, humans, soil, air, and water. Some germs are very dangerous and cause disease. But 95 percent of all germs are harmless. They are actually vital to our health and the health of our planet.

One of the most important jobs of bacteria is to break down material. Billions of microorganisms live in the soil. These tiny organisms feed on all kinds of organic material, or any material that comes from a living thing. Fallen leaves, broken branches, seeds, bones, and skin are a feast for microbes.

Bacteria are also found in animal waste. They play an important role in recycling waste material. They create rich, healthy soil to feed new plants. If bacteria did not do this job, the waste from all the animals on Earth would soon pile up miles high.

Bacteria play an important role inside of us, too. Although we can live without them, our bodies work better with them.

There are trillions of microbes living in our intestines. Most of them are bacteria. They help us digest our food. Just like they break down materials in nature, bacteria help break down food in our bodies. They make minerals and nutrients easier to absorb. Food that is not broken down might leave our bodies before we could use all of it.

"For the first half of geological time our ancestors were bacteria. Most creatures still are bacteria, and each one of our trillions of cells is a colony of bacteria."

—Richard Dawkins

Quick fact

Between 300 and 1,000 different species of bacteria live inside each of us.

↑ *There can be hundreds of millions of microbes in one gram (about the size of a navy bean) of soil.*

Bacteria are also good at using up the extra energy found in sugars and carbohydrates. They can also tell the body to store extra food. Other helpful bacteria keep harmful bacteria from making us sick.

When we take antibiotics, the drugs often kill our good bacteria along with the bad. This in turn can cause problems in our bodies. That is why it is important after taking these drugs to replace the friendly bacteria by eating food like yogurt.

Microorganisms at Work

Other microorganisms have an important role in our lives, too. Throughout the years they have helped us make food, drinks, clothing, and even cleaners.

Yeast are tiny organisms that work very hard. By feeding on sugar and creating gas, they cause breads and cakes to rise. Early settlers knew that by mixing flour and water they could make what is known as bread "starter."

They would leave this mixture at room temperature, watching to see it bubble and rise. This was the natural yeast that live in flour at work.

Most of the starter was used to make bread, but a small bit of dough was kept out. When fresh water and flour was added to this bit of dough, the yeast started to work again. This made a new batch of starter, which could be used to make more bread.

↓Bread starter is a living colony that will stay alive indefinitely if fed every day.

Quick fact

Some bakeries are still using dough made from starter that was first mixed 150 years ago.

Vinegar is a popular ingredient in many foods. It is also used to pickle vegetables so they won't spoil. Some people even use it to clean greasy or dirty surfaces.

Vinegar has been around for thousands of years. Bacteria can turn wine, cider, and fruit juices into vinegar. Different fruits, herbs, and grains make different flavored vinegars.

Wine makers use microbes to create good wine. Yeast causes grapes to ferment. This changes the natural sugars in the fruit into alcohol. The fermented juice is put in big vats to settle. Bacteria help to turn the tart acid in the wine into a milder one. This gives the wine a better flavor.

Did You Know?
Coconut fibers are also separated using bacteria. This fiber, called coir, is used to make ropes and fishing nets.

Linen is a cloth used to make clothing, curtains, tablecloths, and bed sheets. It is made from the flax plant. Stalks of flax are soaked in water. Bacteria in the water eat away at the stalks, leaving the fibers. These fibers are spun into cloth.

How Germs Changed History

Germs played a large part in shaping the population of North America. For thousands of years, Native Americans lived and spread out across the continent. When the first Europeans came, they brought more than a new language and different clothes—they brought germs.

Native Americans had never had any contact with these germs. Their immune systems were unprepared to fight the germs that caused smallpox, influenza, and measles.

↓ *Germs were brought to the New World in food, on clothing, and by people who carried them on their bodies.*

Sometimes explorers and missionaries got sick on the ships on the long trip to North America. Other times they themselves were immune to the germs but still carried them in their bodies. Contact with Europeans was deadly for Native Americans. Diseases spread through the native populations. They killed up to 80 percent of the people.

With many of their people sick and dying, it was difficult for the native tribes to hunt, gather food, and trade with the Europeans. It also made it harder for them to defend their land from the newcomers.

Some people used disease as a way to attack their enemies during war. Ancient armies used to throw dead animal bodies and toxic plants into their enemy's wells. They hoped this would make the opposing army sick.

People who didn't know about germ theory still knew that wounds could become infected. Archers would dip their arrow tips in snake venom, human blood, and animal feces to infect their victims. Before antibiotics, an infected war wound would often lead to amputation or even death for the victim.

The most successful way of using germs in war came with the plague. Armies would drive people sick with the plague ahead of them into enemy lands. Sometimes they would throw diseased bodies over the walls of fortified towns. Launching infected bodies, dead animals, and manure at an enemy became forms of attack.

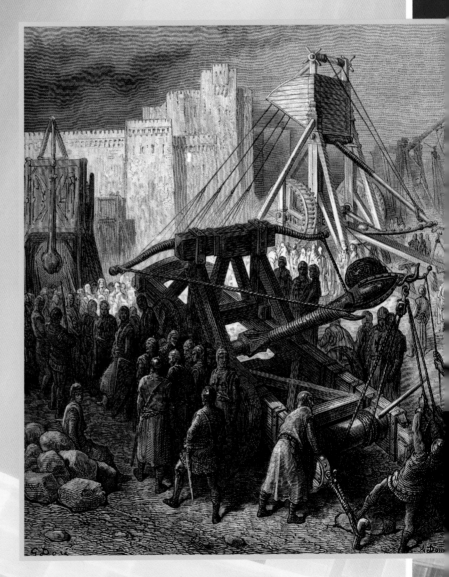

↑Catapults could launch rocks, weapons, and bodies over even the highest walls.

Germs at War

In modern times, germ theory has made biological warfare even more deadly.

During World War I, the German army created strains of anthrax, glanders, cholera, and a wheat fungus to use as weapons. They wanted to weaken or destroy enemy soldiers, their horses, and food supply.

The United States and Britain also studied different viruses to use as weapons during World War II. They stored botulism and anthrax bombs to use against the Germans if the Germans used biological weapons on them.

What's Fair in Warfare?

The Geneva Protocol was a treaty signed in 1925 by 108 nations. It is an agreement among the nations that no one will use chemical or biological weapons in war. Unfortunately, there is no way to prove that these countries are following the rules in the document.

Quick fact

Glanders is an infectious disease that mostly affects horses, mules, and donkeys. It can also spread to humans and is often deadly.

In the Vietnam War, fighters used needle-sharp sticks dipped in feces to stab and cause infections in enemy soldiers.

Today, the biggest danger of biological weapons comes from terrorists. Many countries have laboratories that research the use of germs as weapons. Soldiers today have special training and equipment to use in case of chemical and biological attacks.

There are problems with using biological weapons. Once the germs are released, they are sometimes hard to control. Diseases can spread beyond the area of the enemy. Also, there is danger that the soldiers of the invading army could be infected by their own weapons.

Some germs can be carried by wind or water to the land being attacked. There they can ruin the plants, animals, and even the soil. This can make it impossible to use land that has been captured.

↑The U.S. Army Biological Warfare Laboratories and their projects were stopped in 1969.

A Deadly Accident

A biological warfare research center in Sverdlovsk, Russia, had an accident in 1979. Anthrax was accidentally released from the laboratory. The spores were carried by the wind for miles. Sixty-four people died as well as livestock over 31 miles (50 km) away.

CHAPTER SEVEN

The Cutting Edge

Researchers are always using what they learn about germs to improve our lives. For example, studies have shown that bacteria in our bodies "talk" to each other. Once they enter the body and begin to multiply, they seem to wait. A chemical signal tells them when there are enough bacteria to attack. Scientists are using this knowledge to find a way to block communication among germs.

↑ Scientists study bacteria to learn better ways to control them.

Other bacteria attach themselves to surfaces. Then they join together to create a thin layer of infectious microbes that can coat countertops, doorknobs, or medical instruments. Scientists are working on ways to cover these surfaces with an antibiotic coating that makes it ard for bacteria to stick.

Did You Know?

Silver has been used since ancient times to kill bacteria. Greeks kept wine, water, and vinegar in silver bottles. Silver coins were also dropped in **cisterns** to keep water fresh. Before modern antibiotics, silver **compounds** were put in bandages to prevent infection.

"Every great advance in science has issued from a new audacity of imagination."

— John Dewey; American philosopher, psychologist, and educator; 1929

While viruses cause many diseases, researchers are looking for ways to use the power of these tiny germs. They are using viruses to attack cancer cells.

Many viruses that get into our bodies do not do lasting damage. Reovirus is a germ most of us are exposed to by age five. Our immune systems soon overpower this virus and we recover. Researchers have discovered that this virus grows very well in certain tumor cells. They can make the virus avoid healthy cells. Instead, it looks for a host in cancer cells and grows rapidly. Eventually the cancer cells explode and are destroyed.

Other tests use certain plant viruses as "smart bombs." These viruses are given special signal proteins on their outside shell. These proteins then hunt for particular cells, such as cancer cells. Once the virus enters a cell, it releases its cargo. Scientists hope they can use this virus to bring cancer drugs directly into cancer cells without harming healthy cells.

→ Viruses attack a cancer cell.

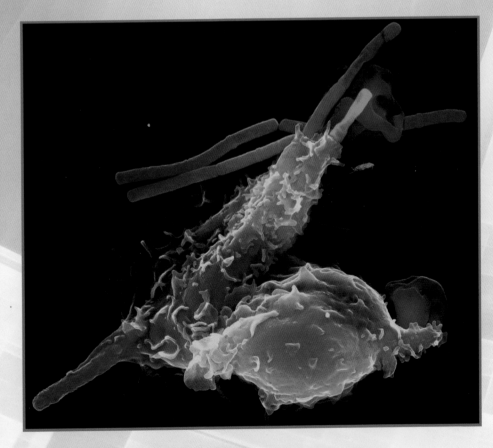

Germs Help the Planet

Researchers are also discovering that some molds may help solve fuel shortages.

Biodiesel is a type of fuel made from plant oils rather than from petroleum. Using plants such as soybeans to get oil is expensive and requires farmland. With less farmland used for growing food, food prices rise. Molds do not need soil or large spaces to grow. They can grow in tanks. Someday they may be a cheap, renewable source for **biofuels**.

Scientists are also using yeast for biofuel production. Yeast turns plant material into ethanol, which is then used for fuel. A new type of yeast can turn leftover plant materials such as stalks and straw into fuel.

Using microbes to turn plants into fuel allows more fields to be used for growing food. This helps keep food supplies up and prices down.

→ *There are thousands of species of molds.*

Scientists are using their growing knowledge of viruses to better understand the sudden death of bee colonies.

Since 2006, bee colonies across North America have collapsed. Bees are a very important part of the plant life cycle. As they collect nectar, they **pollinate** thousands of different types of plants. Bees play a role in producing at least one-third of our food. Scientists believe both a virus and a fungus are attacking the bee colonies at the same time.

Another virus seems to be attacking frogs in the United Kingdom. Researchers have noticed huge population crashes from infection. The disease seems to have started in the southern part of England and moved north. Scientists want to find out how this virus is passed along. This will help them figure out how to stop the spread of the virus.

Quick fact

The new bee virus may be related to one that wiped out bee populations in India 20 years ago.

The Future of Germ Research

Microbiologists study tiny life forms such as parasites, bacteria, and protozoa. Understanding the mysterious ways of these creatures is helping scientists develop better vaccines and other helpful drugs.

For example, scientists are studying worms that cause diseases such as elephantiasis and river blindness. They noticed that these microorganisms could change their behavior depending on their hosts' immune systems. If the immune system was strong, the worms could speed up their reproduction. Then they could attack more quickly.

This means that ordinary vaccines may not fight these types of diseases. Vaccines make the immune system react quicker. This may actually have a harmful effect with some diseases. It may cause the viruses that carry them to spread. More research is being done to discover which treatments are best at killing these microbes.

→ Viruses are passed to a victim from a mosquito through saliva from its bite.

Arbovirus Bites

Arbovirus is short for **ar**thropod-**bo**rne virus. These viruses are passed along mainly by **arthropods** such as mosquitoes. When mosquitoes bite, they transfer some infected blood into each victim. The virus then finds host cells and begins to grow and spread.

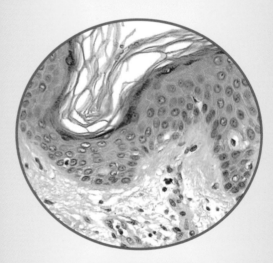

Scientists have recently discovered a new pathogen. It is different from the four types of known germs. These are particles known as **prions**.

Like viruses, prions cannot reproduce by themselves. They mostly infect humans and large animals like cattle. Prions are abnormal proteins. They enter a healthy organism and cause other proteins in the body to become abnormal too. This produces a large amount of prions.

Prions attack the brain and nerves. They kill many cells in the brain. The dead cells form holes inside the brain, making it look like a sponge.

Research on this new type of infectious particle is just beginning. So far, any diseases caused by prions are untreatable and deadly.

As scientists study germs more closely, they begin to unravel the mysteries of this microscopic world teeming with life. New discoveries will continue to give us a better understanding of our own bodies and the love-hate relationship we have with germs.

↓ *Researchers are working hard to find new cures for diseases.*

Quick fact

One disease caused by prions is known as mad cow disease. In humans it is called Creutzfeldt-Jakob disease (CJD).

Timeline

460 B.C. Hippocrates believes diseases have a natural cause when the four humors are not in balance in the body.

50 B.C. Varro writes that tiny "animalcules" may cause disease.

1500 Paracelsus believes disease is caused by toxins in food and space. He uses chemicals to try to cure sickness.

1546 Girolamo Fracastoro writes that diseases are caused by invisible spores.

1665 Robert Hooke publishes his book *Micrographia*, showing drawings made using a microscope.

1668 Francesco Redi performs his experiments on meat, disproving spontaneous regeneration.

1674 Antonie van Leeuwenhoek observes the first microorganisms in water.

1798 Edward Jenner uses cowpox inoculation to prevent smallpox.

1847 Ignaz Semmelweis reduces deaths from childbed fever by having doctors wash their hands before examining patients.

1849 John Snow has a London water pump shut off to prevent the spread of cholera.

1865 Louis Pasteur writes a paper on pasteurization.

1867 Joseph Lister uses carbolic acid to prevent wound infections.

1876 Robert Koch proves anthrax is caused by bacteria.

1898 Marinus Beijerinck suggests a link between virus and cancer.

1928	Alexander Fleming discovers *Penicillium notatum*.
1935	Wendell Stanley crystallizes the tobacco mosaic virus.
1942	Doctors begin testing penicillin on humans.
1969	U.S. Army Biological Warfare Laboratories are closed.
1979	A biological warfare research center in Russia accidentally releases anthrax from its laboratory, killing 64 people.
1979	Smallpox becomes the first infectious disease to be wiped out.
1983	HIV, the virus that causes AIDS, is identified.
2006	Scientists believe a virus is causing the collapse of bee colonies across North America.
2010	The World Health Organization declares that the H1N1 (swine flu) pandemic, which began in Mexico in 2009, is officially over.

Glossary

amputations Removing arms or legs because of infection

anatomy The structure of the body

anthrax A highly infectious animal disease

antibacterial Any drug that destroys bacteria or affects their growth

antigens Components of a microorganism that cause the body's immune system to react

antisepsis Stopping the growth of harmful organisms with a germ-killing substance

antiviral Acting to make a virus ineffective

archaeologists People who study ancient people through fossils, remains, and artifacts

arthropod Insect, spider, or crab with jointed legs and hard exoskeleton

attenuated Reduced in strength

biofuels Fuels made from a renewable resource

biological About life and living things

bloodletting Medical treatment where blood is taken from the patient

carbolic acid A liquid used to disinfect

cistern A tank built to catch and store rainwater

compound A combination of two or more different atoms or elements

contaminated Impure

crystallize To form a solid from something that is dissolved in a liquid

dormant Inactive, resting

elasticity How easily something can go back to its original shape

epidemic An outbreak of a disease that affects many people

genetic Inherited through genes

immune system The system that protects the body from disease and infection

infectious Easily spread

inoculating Injecting microorganisms or viruses to bring on immunity

intestines The passage in our body where food is digested

isolating Separating something from others

leeching Seeping through

maggots Larvae of flies

microbes Germs or other living things too small to be seen without a microscope

mosaic Pattern of connecting pieces

mummified Treated with chemicals to prevent rotting

mystical Spiritual

optical Designed to aid sight

pandemic An epidemic over a large area

parasites Animals or plants that get food by living on or in another animal or plant

pathogens Harmful microorganisms

plague A very serious disease that spreads quickly to many people and often causes death

pneumonia Disease where fluid fills infected lungs

polio Disease where the nerves of the brain and spinal cord swell

pollinate Fertilize by applying pollen

prions Infectious particles made mostly of protein

protists Single-celled organisms including amoebas, paramecia, and some algae

regeneration Growing anew

resistance The ability to not be affected by something

sanitation Systems for cleaning water and getting rid of sewage

spontaneous Happening suddenly as if without cause

spores Plant cells that develop into new plants

supernatural Not from the natural world

surgical For medical procedures involving an operation

symptoms Changes from the normal that show someone is sick

tumor An abnormal growth of tissue

yeast A yellow fungus used to make bread dough rise and to ferment alcoholic drinks

For More Information

Books

Claybourne, Anna. **World's Worst Germs: Microorganisms and Disease.** Heinemann-Raintree, 2005.

Farrell, Jeanette. **Invisible Allies: Microbes That Shape Our Lives**. Farrar, Straus and Giroux, 2005.

Morgan, Sally. **Germ Killers: Fighting Disease.** Heinemann Library, 2009.

Wearing, Judy. **Bacteria: Strep, Clostridium, and Other Bacteria.** Crabtree Publishing, 2010.

Websites

Kids Health: What Are Germs?
http://kidshealth.org/teen/index.jsp?tracking=T_Home
KidsHealth is the most-visited website for children's health and development. Find out what types of germs there are, what germs do, and how you can protect yourself from germs.

Digital Learning Center for Microbial Ecology
http://commtechlab.msu.edu/sites/dlc-me/
Visit the microbe zoo to discover microscopic organisms and the habitats in which they live. This site includes stories from newspapers and magazines related to microbiology and profiles of microbiologists.

Cells Alive! www.cellsalive.com
Watch interactive animations of cell cycles, meiosis, and mitosis.

Biology4Kids www.biology4kids.com/files/micro_main.html
Take a look at the world of microbes, including bacteria, fungi, algae, and protozoa.

Easy Kids Science Experiments
www.easy-kids-science-experiments.com/microbiology-science-projects.html
Check out this site for microbiology science experiments about bacteria, fungi, viruses, yeast, and more.

Microbe World www.microbeworld.org
Visit Microbe World to read all about the latest microbial discoveries in news articles, featured videos, and audio and video podcasts.

The Kids Science Zone www.kidssciencezone.com/microbiology
Science 2.0 created this website to bring readers accurate and objective articles about science.

I Love Bacteria http://ilovebacteria.com/index.html
Visit the home of the geekiest science stuff on the Net. Ask a silly question or try these experiments at home.

Science Kids www.sciencekids.co.nz/quizzes/biology.html
Science Kids brings science and technology together. Check out the fun experiments, games, facts, and quizzes.

Index